The Olympics

John Escott

Series Editors: Steve Barlow and Steve Skidmore

GINN

Published by Ginn and Company
Halley Court, Jordan Hill, Oxford OX2 8EJ
A division of Reed Educational and Professional Publishing Ltd
Telephone number for ordering **Impact**: 01865 888084

OXFORD   MELBOURNE   AUCKLAND   JOHANNESBURG   BLANTYRE
GABORONE   IBADAN   PORTSMOUTH (NH) USA   CHICAGO

First published 1999

2003 2002 2001 2000 99

10 9 8 7 6 5 4 3 2 1

ISBN 0 435 21233 8

Illustrations
Karen Hiscock

Picture research
Helen Reilly

Cover artwork
Chris Swee / The Organisation

Designed by Shireen Nathoo Design

Printed and bound in Spain by Eldelvives

Acknowledgements
The Author and Publishers wish to thank the following for permission
to reproduce photographs on the pages noted:
Simon Bruty/Allsport pp.3, 4, 43; Hewitt/Allsport p.5a; Michael Steele/Empics pp.5b, 13;
Allsport pp.3, 6, 7, 10, 14, 23, 24a, 26, 27a, 44a, b, 30, 33c, 35, 48; Empics Ltd pp.6b,
12; Popperfoto pp.11, 28, 38b; Richard Massa/Allsport p.15; Gary Prior/Allsport pp.16,
20; C.Dunn/Allsport pp.3, 17; Tony Marshall/Empics pp.18, 32c, 33a,b; Tony
Duffy/Allsport pp.19, 45; Steve Powell/Allsport pp3, 21; Allsport Historical Collection
p.22a; Neal Simpson/Empics pp.3, 22b, 24b; Matthew Ashton/Empics p.25; Michael
Cooper/Allsport p.27b; Pic Witters/Empics p.29; Steven E.Sutton/Colorsport p.31; Mike
Powell/Allsport p.32a; Jamie Squire/Allsport pp.32b, 34b; Gray Mortimore/Allsport pp.3,
34a,c, 37; AP p.36; Spooner pp.40-41; Brian Rybolt/Impact pp.3, 38a, 39.

Contents

Introduction

The world's greatest sportsmen and women gather to compete against each other every four years. They aim to prove they are the best in the world at their chosen sport. They will not win money for their efforts. They hope to win medals.

Most competitors will return home empty-handed. But they will be happy just to have taken part in the greatest festival of sport – the Olympic Games!

Millions of people follow the events on television. They want to see the athletes live up to the Olympic motto:

"Faster ...

... higher ...

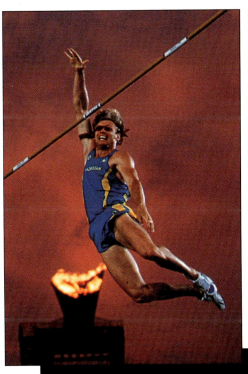

Did you know?

There is more than one type of Olympic Games.

There are:
• The Summer Olympics
• The Winter Olympics
• The Special Olympics
• The Paralympics.

... stronger!"

Olympic sports

The first modern Olympic Games were held in 1896. At these Games, only nine sports were contested. Nowadays, Olympic hopefuls can try for the gold medal in over 30 events!

▲ *Malcolm Cooper, of Britain, won a shooting gold in both 1984 and 1988.*

▲ *Chris Boardman won a cycling gold for Britain in Barcelona in 1992.*

▲ *The British Men's hockey team won gold in Seoul in 1988.*

◄ *Britain's Steve Redgrave and Matt Pinsent won gold for rowing in Barcelona in 1992.*

How the Olympics started

The first recorded ancient Olympic Games were held in the year 776BCE.

The first Olympic village was in Olympia in Greece. This is where the word 'Olympic' comes from.

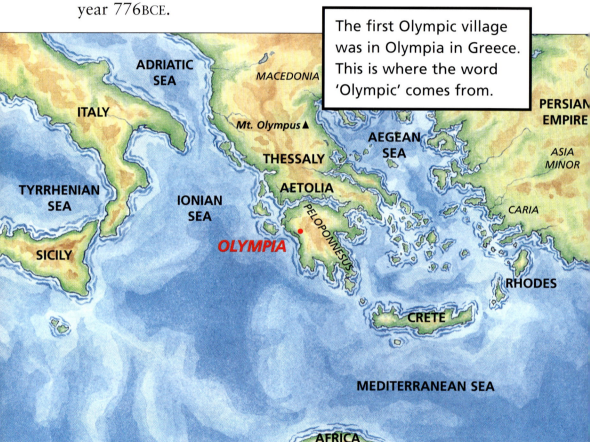

All wars throughout the Greek Empire were stopped when the Games were played. This allowed the athletes to travel safely to the Games from their homes.

Only male Greek citizens could compete at the ancient Games. No women were allowed to watch or enter them.

The earliest Games had only one event. It was a race of about 200 metres across the stadium. The distance was called a 'stade', which is where the word 'stadium' comes from.

The first recorded Olympic champion to win the race was a young cook. His prize was a crown made from olive tree branches.

◄ Winners were rewarded only with a crown cut from olive tree branches.

Gradually, more events were added to the Games. These were:

- other races
- a five-event competition which involved running, long jump, discus, javelin and wrestling
- boxing
- chariot races.

The ancient Olympic Games continued for about 1000 years. They were banned in 393CE by a Roman emperor called Theodosius.

The modern Olympics

The Games started again in 1896. A Frenchman called
Baron Pierre de Coubertin believed that sport could bring
nations closer together. He formed an International Olympic
Committee. It agreed to hold an international sports
competition every four years.

Pierre de Coubertin

The first modern Olympic Games were held in Athens. Thirteen countries and 311 athletes took part – most of them from Greece. The Games were a great success.

In 1900, the Olympics were held in Paris. More than 1000 athletes entered from 22 countries. For the first time, women were allowed to compete.

Rudolf Bauer won the discus ▶ gold for Hungary in 1900.

Did you know?

Since 1896, the summer games have been cancelled three times.

In **1916** Berlin was due to host the Games but they were cancelled because of the First World War.

In **1940** and **1944** the Second World War meant the Games could not be held.

Olympic legends

JESSE OWENS
Hero of the 1936 games

Jesse Owens was born in Alabama, USA in 1913. He had ten brothers and sisters.

He won four gold medals at the 1936 Berlin Olympics.

He won the:
- 100 metres
- 200 metres
- long jump
- 4 x 400 metres relay

The 1936 Games have often been called the Nazi Olympics because they took place in Hitler's Germany. Adolf Hitler was furious at Owens' success because the athlete was black. Hitler believed that white people were better than any other race. Owens proved him wrong.

CARL LEWIS
An Olympic superstar!

Carl Lewis was born in Alabama, USA in 1961.

In the 1984 Games, he won the same four events that Jessie Owens had won in 1936.

Lewis also won the gold for long jump at four Olympic Games.

Overall, he has won nine Olympic gold medals. He is one of the greatest athletes of modern times.

He won:

Los Angeles, 1984
- 100 metres
- 200 metres
- long jump
- 4 x 100 metres relay

Seoul, 1988
- 100 metres
- long jump

Barcelona, 1992
- long jump
- 4 x 100 metres relay

Atlanta, 1996
- long jump

13

Olympic symbols

The Olympic flag was first used in 1914. It shows five linked rings. They stand for the coming together of the five continents of the world: America, Europe, Asia, Africa and Australasia.

The five colours of the rings also have a special meaning. The flag of every nation in the world contains one or more of these five colours.

The Olympic flame was first used in the modern Olympics in 1928. It is lit at the opening ceremony and burns throughout the Games.

The torch is usually lit by rays from the sun in Olympia in Greece. This is where the Olympic Games were first held. The flame is then passed from torch to torch by relays of runners. Huge crowds watch it reach the city where the Olympics are being held.

Hot facts

The torch relay began in 1936 at the Berlin Games.

For the 1976 Montreal Games, a laser beam was sent from Greece to light a torch in Canada.

At the 1992 Barcelona Games, the Olympic flame was lit by an archer shooting a burning arrow.

The torch in the USA relay for the 1996 Olympics.

At the opening ceremony of the Games, a competitor from the host country makes the Olympic Promise:

"In the name of all competitors, I promise that we will take part in these Olympic Games, respecting and abiding by the rules which govern them, in the true spirit of sportsmanship, for the glory of sport and the honour of our teams."

The opening ceremony of the 1998 Winter Olympics in Japan.

No competitor is paid by the Olympic Committee to appear in the Games. There is no prize money. The only prizes are medals – bronze for third place, silver for second and gold for coming first. But medals are more important than money for most competitors. Their dream is to be an Olympic champion.

Did you know?

An Olympic gold medal isn't really made from gold. It is made from solid silver and covered with gold leaf.

Bronze medals have only been awarded since the 1908 Games.

◀ *Gold, silver and bronze medals from the Olympic Games of 1996.*

Athletics

Athletics is the largest group of sports in the Olympics. It covers all the track and field events. To win an athletics Olympic medal you need to be good at throwing, running and jumping.

Throwing ...

Tessa Sanderson won the gold for Britain in the women's javelin in 1984.

Running ...

Roger Black won the men's 400 metres silver medal at the 1996 Atlanta Games.

Jumping …

Jonathan Edwards won the triple jump silver medal in Atlanta in 1996.

Britain's Daley Thompson was good at throwing, running and jumping!
He won the men's decathlon gold medal in 1980 and 1984. To win gold,
Thompson had to compete in ten events in just two days.

WHAT A FLOP!

The American high jumper, Dick Fosbury, created a new style of high jumping. At the 1968 Mexico Olympics, he hurled himself backwards rather than forwards, over the bar. He beat the Olympic record by 6.4 centimetres and won the gold medal. This style of jumping is now known as the 'Fosbury Flop'.

▲ *A successful flop!*

FAST!

The 100 metres sprint lasts only ten seconds and each athlete takes only about 35 strides. But it takes years of hard training to win the Olympic gold and the title of fastest man or woman on the planet!

◄ *Britain's Linford Christie won gold in the 100 metres sprint in 1992.*

LONG!

One of the most famous races in the Olympics is the marathon. It is run in memory of a Greek messenger who lived in 490BCE. He ran 280 km to Athens with a message that the Greeks had won a battle on the Plain of Marathon. When he arrived he announced, "Rejoice! We conquer!" It was the last thing he said. He was so tired that he dropped down dead.

Nowadays the marathon is 26 miles and 385 yards (42 km) long. This strange distance came about because the 1908 Marathon was run from Windsor Castle to the White City Stadium in London – a distance of exactly 42 km.

The first runner into the stadium in the 1908 marathon was called Dorando Pietri. He was disqualified because he collapsed and received help to cross the line. Queen Alexandra felt so sorry for him that she awarded him a special prize.

In the pool

Swimming is the second largest sport in the Olympics. There are 16 different swimming events for both men and women. They include individual races in freestyle (crawl), breaststroke, backstroke and butterfly. There are also medley races of all four strokes.

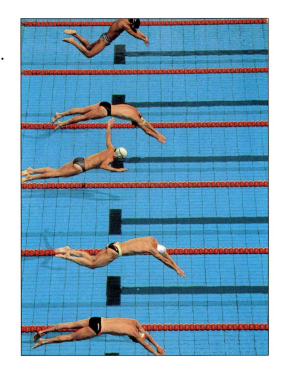

WATER POLO

One of the toughest team games takes place in the pool. Each water polo team has seven players. They must be good swimmers and skilful passers. Only the goalkeeper can hold the ball with both hands.

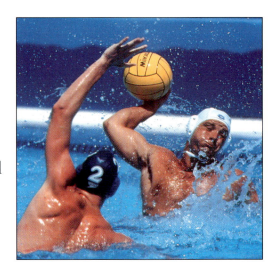

DIVING

The diving in the Olympics is dramatic. Highboard diving first began in 1904. Competitors dive from a 10-metre high board. Diving from a springboard started in the 1908 Olympics.

Britain's Lesley Ward diving in the 1992 Barcelona Games.

Boxing

Boxing is one of the world's oldest sports. It was one of the events in the ancient Olympic Games. It has been part of the modern Olympics since 1908.

There are 12 weight classes in the Games. These range from light flyweight (a boxer can weigh up to a maximum 48kg) to super heavyweight (minimum weight 91kg).

Teofilo Stevenson ▶ of Cuba is the only man to have won three Olympic heavyweight gold medals – in 1972, 1976 and 1980.

Did you know?

A punch is counted only if a fighter hits his opponent with the white area of the boxing glove. The fights are a maximum of three rounds, each lasting three minutes. If there is no knockout, the winner is decided by five judges.

FROM OLYMPIC GOLD TO WORLD CHAMPION

Many amateur boxers use the Olympic Games as a stepping stone to becoming a professional fighter.

Seven men have won an Olympic boxing gold medal and gone on to be the professional world champions. These include Cassius Clay and Lennox Lewis.

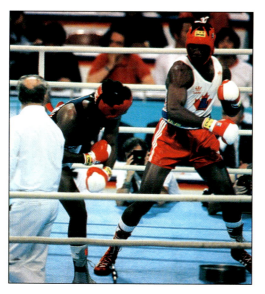

◄ *Lennox Lewis won gold in the 1988 super heavyweight final.*

Did you know?

Cassius Clay threw away the gold medal he won in 1960. He hurled it into the River Ohio because he was so disgusted at the way black people were being treated in America.

Clay later changed his name to Muhammad Ali. Ali's medal was replaced after he lit the Olympic flame at the 1996 Atlanta Games.

Basketball

Basketball is one of the world's most popular team games. It became an Olympic sport in 1936. The USA have been champions at every Games except in 1972 and 1988.

The 1972 final will always be remembered for its exciting ending. The American team were playing the USSR. The USSR were winning 49–48.

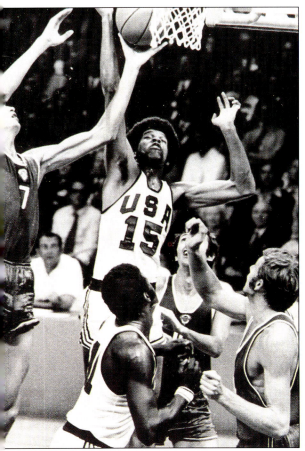

With three seconds left to play, the USA scored two free throws to take a 50–49 lead. The buzzer sounded for the end of the game.

However, the match clock showed one second of time still remaining. The referee ordered this to be played. Play started and the buzzer sounded again. The Americans went wild – they thought they were Olympic champions.

◄ *The exciting 1972 final.*

However, the timekeepers had made a mistake. There were *still* three seconds left to play. The court was cleared and the players got ready to play the final moments. One of the Russian players threw the ball the whole length of the court. It was caught by Alexander Belov. He leapt past two Americans and dropped the ball in the basket – for two points! The buzzer sounded and the Russians had won by 51–50.

Since 1992, America has played 'dream teams' in the Olympic basketball competition. Stars such as Magic Johnson and Michael Jordan played for the American side. They helped the team to win gold medals easily.

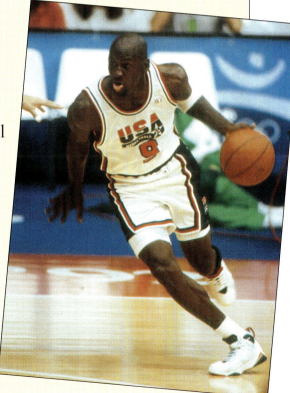

Michael Jordan in the 1992 ► *dream team.*

The Winter Olympics

The fastest Olympic champions are not the athletes of the Summer Games. They are the men and women who speed across snow and ice on skis, sledges and skates. They are the athletes of the Winter Olympics.

▲ *Skiers can reach speeds of over 100 kilometres an hour.*

Ice hockey and figure skating once took place in the early Summer Olympics. It was then decided to hold a separate Winter and Summer Games. The first Winter Olympics were held in 1924 in Chamonix, France.

The record for winning the most gold medals at one Winter Games is held by an American, Eric Heiden. He won five gold medals for speed skating at the 1980 Games at Lake Placid.

▲ *Eric Heiden, the speed skater.*

Did you know?

The only man so far to win a gold medal in both the Summer and Winter Games is Edward Eagen. He won the 1920 light heavyweight boxing gold and was also a member of the American four-man bobsleigh team.

The Winter Olympics are a spectacle of speed, power and beauty.

▲ The Biathlon – competitors have to be good at cross-country skiing and shooting.

▲ Ice hockey is one of the toughest Olympic team games.

▲ Great Britain won the four-man
bobsleigh bronze medal at
Nagano in 1998.

▲ Snow-boarding first
appeared in the 1998
Winter Olympics.

▲ How would you fancy jumping off a mountainside?
That's what ski jumpers do!

The Paralympics

The Paralympics are Games for people who have physical difficulties. There are events for:

- people in wheelchairs
- people who are blind or cannot see very well
- people who have had arms or legs amputated
- people with cerebral palsy.

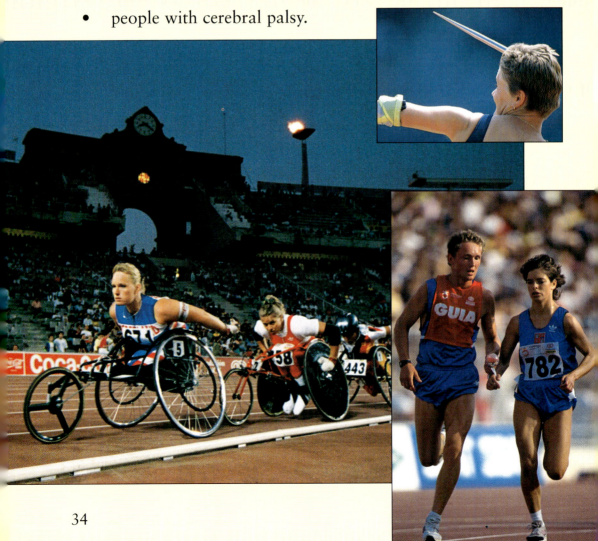

The opening of the 1996 Paralympics in Atlanta.

1996 ATLANTA PAR
THE TRIUMPH OF THE HUMAN SPIRIT

Did you know?

The Paralympics is the second largest sports event in the world.

At the 1996 Atlanta Games, nearly 5,000 athletes from over 100 countries competed.

There are both Summer and Winter Paralympics. The Paralympics take place in the same city as the main Olympic Games. The first international Games for people with physical difficulties were held in England in 1948. The first Paralympics were held in Rome in 1960.

There are over 15 Paralympic sports for athletes to compete in. Events include:

- wheelchair discus and shot putt
- track and field
- long jump
- swimming
- wheelchair basketball
- basketball
- tennis
- ice sledge.

◄Anne Mette Samdal won the 100 metres ice sledge speed race at the 1998 Olympics in Japan.

TANNI GREY
Hero of the 1992 Games

Tanni Grey is one of Britain's most successful athletes. She is a wheelchair sprinter and takes part in long distance events. She has won the following medals:

1992 Barcelona
- 100 metres gold
- 200 metres gold
- 400 metres gold
- 800 metres gold

1996 Atlanta
- 800 metres gold
- 100 metres silver
- 200 metres silver
- 400 metres silver

I was about eighteen when I discovered I had a natural talent for track events. I began to train seriously. You have to enjoy sport, and especially your particular event. I train four or five hours every day, including weekends.

Tanni's dedication helped her reach the top of her sport. She was rewarded with Olympic medals, and an MBE for her services to sport.

The Special Olympics

The Special Olympics are for children and adults who have learning difficulties. The Special Olympics were first held in 1968 in Chicago, USA. Around 7,000 athletes from 150 countries competed.

The Special Olympic Oath

The Special Olympics has its own oath:
"Let me win. But if I cannot, let me be brave in the attempt."

Trouble at the Olympics

POLITICS

The Games are meant to bring nations closer together. But because so many people watch the Olympics on the television, the Games have been used to make political points.

The worst incident happened in 1972 at the Munich Games.

Eight Arab terrorists broke into the Israeli team's headquarters. They shot dead a wrestling coach and a weightlifter. Some Israeli athletes escaped, but nine were taken hostage.

The Games were suspended and the Olympic village was surrounded by 12,000 police.

Later that day, the security forces tried to make a rescue attempt. In the following gun battle, all nine Israeli hostages were shot dead. Five terrorists and one policeman were also killed.

◄A terrorist keeping watch at the Munich Olympics in 1972.

DRUGS

Some people want to win a gold medal at any cost. So they take drugs to help their performance. Because of this, strict drugs testing takes place at the Olympics.

If competitors refuse to take a drugs test or are found guilty of taking drugs, they are banned from the Games. Over 50 competitors have been caught taking drugs at the modern Olympics.

Ben Johnson of Canada came first in the men's 100 metres final in 1988. He set a new world record and beat his great rival, Carl Lewis of the USA.

After the race, Johnson took a drugs test. It was positive. Next day his gold medal was taken away and awarded to Lewis. Johnson was sent home in disgrace and banned from athletics for four years.

Ben Johnson won gold in 1988 with the help of drugs.

More Olympic legends

EMIL ZATOPEK
One of the greatest long-distance runners

Emil Zatopek was born in the Czech republic in 1922.

He won the 10,000 metres gold medal at the 1948 Olympics in London. Four years later, at the Helsinki Games, he won three gold medals.

He won the:
- 5,000 metres
- 10,000 metres
- marathon

OLGA KORBUT
The smiling gymnast

Olga Korbut was born in 1956.

She started out as a reserve for the Russian gymnastics team at the 1972 Olympics in Munich. Then one of the team fell ill and Olga took her place.

She won three gold medals and one silver:
- individual beam
- individual floor
- whole team
- parallel bars (silver)

MARK SPITZ
The greatest Olympic swimmer

Mark Spitz was born in 1950 in the USA.

In 1968 he was called a failure because he was expected to win six golds at the Mexico City Games. Instead, he won two golds, a bronze and a silver.

Four years later Spitz made up for this 'failure'. He won seven gold medals at the Munich Games. This is still a record for the most gold medals won by one person at an Olympics.

Spitz also broke the world record in every one of his final races:

- 100 and 200 metres freestyle
- 100 and 200 metres butterfly
- 4 x 100 metres freestyle relay
- 4 x 200 metres freestyle relay
- 4 x 100 metres medley relay

Where it all happened

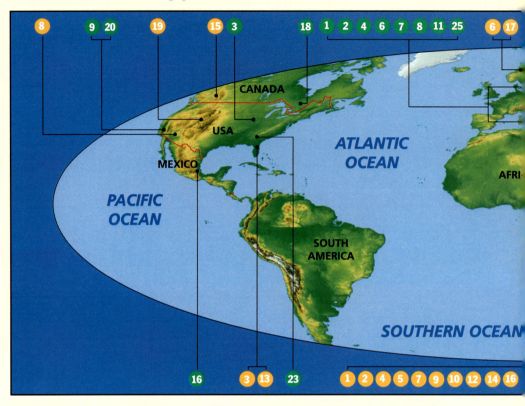

SUMMER GAMES

1	1896	Athens
2	1900	Paris
3	1904	St Louis
4	1908	London
5	1912	Stockholm
6	1920	Antwerp
7	1924	Paris
8	1928	Amsterdam
9	1932	Los Angeles
10	1936	Berlin
11	1948	London
12	1952	Helsinki
13	1956	Melbourne
14	1960	Rome
15	1964	Tokyo
16	1968	Mexico City
17	1972	Munich
18	1976	Montreal
19	1980	Moscow
20	1984	Los Angeles
21	1988	Seoul
22	1992	Barcelona
23	1996	Atlanta

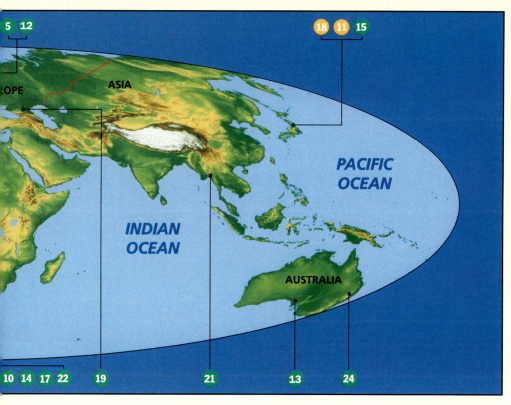

24	2000	Sydney	8	1960	Squaw Valley
25	2004	Athens	9	1964	Innsbruck
			10	1968	Grenoble
			11	1972	Sapporo
			12	1976	Innsbruck
WINTER GAMES			13	1980	Lake Placid
1	1924	Chamonix	14	1984	Sarajevo
2	1928	St Moritz	15	1988	Calgary
3	1932	Lake Placid	16	1992	Albertville
4	1936	Garmisch	17	1993	Lillehammer
5	1948	St Moritz	18	1998	Nagano
6	1952	Oslo	19	2002	Salt Lake City
7	1956	Cortina			

Index

"The important thing in the Olympic Games is not winning but taking part. The essential thing in life is not conquering but fighting well."
Pierre de Coubertin, founder of the modern Olympic Games